THE COMP

RUNNERS

DAY-BY-DAY LOG
2012 CALENDAR

**Andrews McMeel
Publishing, LLC**

Kansas City • Sydney • London

MARTY JEROME

2011

January
S	M	T	W	T	F	S
						1
2	3	4	5	6	7	8
9	10	11	12	13	14	15
16	17	18	19	20	21	22
23	24	25	26	27	28	29
30	31					

February
S	M	T	W	T	F	S
		1	2	3	4	5
6	7	8	9	10	11	12
13	14	15	16	17	18	19
20	21	22	23	24	25	26
27	28					

March
S	M	T	W	T	F	S
		1	2	3	4	5
6	7	8	9	10	11	12
13	14	15	16	17	18	19
20	21	22	23	24	25	26
27	28	29	30	31		

April
S	M	T	W	T	F	S
					1	2
3	4	5	6	7	8	9
10	11	12	13	14	15	16
17	18	19	20	21	22	23
24	25	26	27	28	29	30

May
S	M	T	W	T	F	S
1	2	3	4	5	6	7
8	9	10	11	12	13	14
15	16	17	18	19	20	21
22	23	24	25	26	27	28
29	30	31				

June
S	M	T	W	T	F	S
			1	2	3	4
5	6	7	8	9	10	11
12	13	14	15	16	17	18
19	20	21	22	23	24	25
26	27	28	29	30		

July
S	M	T	W	T	F	S
					1	2
3	4	5	6	7	8	9
10	11	12	13	14	15	16
17	18	19	20	21	22	23
24	25	26	27	28	29	30
31						

August
S	M	T	W	T	F	S
	1	2	3	4	5	6
7	8	9	10	11	12	13
14	15	16	17	18	19	20
21	22	23	24	25	26	27
28	29	30	31			

September
S	M	T	W	T	F	S
				1	2	3
4	5	6	7	8	9	10
11	12	13	14	15	16	17
18	19	20	21	22	23	24
25	26	27	28	29	30	

October
S	M	T	W	T	F	S
						1
2	3	4	5	6	7	8
9	10	11	12	13	14	15
16	17	18	19	20	21	22
23	24	25	26	27	28	29
30	31					

November
S	M	T	W	T	F	S
		1	2	3	4	5
6	7	8	9	10	11	12
13	14	15	16	17	18	19
20	21	22	23	24	25	26
27	28	29	30			

December
S	M	T	W	T	F	S
				1	2	3
4	5	6	7	8	9	10
11	12	13	14	15	16	17
18	19	20	21	22	23	24
25	26	27	28	29	30	31

2013

January
S	M	T	W	T	F	S
		1	2	3	4	5
6	7	8	9	10	11	12
13	14	15	16	17	18	19
20	21	22	23	24	25	26
27	28	29	30	31		

February
S	M	T	W	T	F	S
					1	2
3	4	5	6	7	8	9
10	11	12	13	14	15	16
17	18	19	20	21	22	23
24	25	26	27	28		

March
S	M	T	W	T	F	S
					1	2
3	4	5	6	7	8	9
10	11	12	13	14	15	16
17	18	19	20	21	22	23
24	25	26	27	28	29	30
31						

April
S	M	T	W	T	F	S
	1	2	3	4	5	6
7	8	9	10	11	12	13
14	15	16	17	18	19	20
21	22	23	24	25	26	27
28	29	30				

May
S	M	T	W	T	F	S
			1	2	3	4
5	6	7	8	9	10	11
12	13	14	15	16	17	18
19	20	21	22	23	24	25
26	27	28	29	30	31	

June
S	M	T	W	T	F	S
						1
2	3	4	5	6	7	8
9	10	11	12	13	14	15
16	17	18	19	20	21	22
23	24	25	26	27	28	29
30						

July
S	M	T	W	T	F	S
	1	2	3	4	5	6
7	8	9	10	11	12	13
14	15	16	17	18	19	20
21	22	23	24	25	26	27
28	29	30	31			

August
S	M	T	W	T	F	S
				1	2	3
4	5	6	7	8	9	10
11	12	13	14	15	16	17
18	19	20	21	22	23	24
25	26	27	28	29	30	31

September
S	M	T	W	T	F	S
1	2	3	4	5	6	7
8	9	10	11	12	13	14
15	16	17	18	19	20	21
22	23	24	25	26	27	28
29	30					

October
S	M	T	W	T	F	S
		1	2	3	4	5
6	7	8	9	10	11	12
13	14	15	16	17	18	19
20	21	22	23	24	25	26
27	28	29	30	31		

November
S	M	T	W	T	F	S
					1	2
3	4	5	6	7	8	9
10	11	12	13	14	15	16
17	18	19	20	21	22	23
24	25	26	27	28	29	30

December
S	M	T	W	T	F	S
1	2	3	4	5	6	7
8	9	10	11	12	13	14
15	16	17	18	19	20	21
22	23	24	25	26	27	28
29	30	31				

2012

January

S	M	T	W	T	F	S
1	2	3	4	5	6	7
8	9	10	11	12	13	14
15	16	17	18	19	20	21
22	23	24	25	26	27	28
29	30	31				

February

S	M	T	W	T	F	S
			1	2	3	4
5	6	7	8	9	10	11
12	13	14	15	16	17	18
19	20	21	22	23	24	25
26	27	28	29			

March

S	M	T	W	T	F	S
				1	2	3
4	5	6	7	8	9	10
11	12	13	14	15	16	17
18	19	20	21	22	23	24
25	26	27	28	29	30	31

April

S	M	T	W	T	F	S
1	2	3	4	5	6	7
8	9	10	11	12	13	14
15	16	17	18	19	20	21
22	23	24	25	26	27	28
29	30					

May

S	M	T	W	T	F	S
		1	2	3	4	5
6	7	8	9	10	11	12
13	14	15	16	17	18	19
20	21	22	23	24	25	26
27	28	29	30	31		

June

S	M	T	W	T	F	S
					1	2
3	4	5	6	7	8	9
10	11	12	13	14	15	16
17	18	19	20	21	22	23
24	25	26	27	28	29	30

July

S	M	T	W	T	F	S
1	2	3	4	5	6	7
8	9	10	11	12	13	14
15	16	17	18	19	20	21
22	23	24	25	26	27	28
29	30	31				

August

S	M	T	W	T	F	S
			1	2	3	4
5	6	7	8	9	10	11
12	13	14	15	16	17	18
19	20	21	22	23	24	25
26	27	28	29	30	31	

September

S	M	T	W	T	F	S
						1
2	3	4	5	6	7	8
9	10	11	12	13	14	15
16	17	18	19	20	21	22
23	24	25	26	27	28	29
30						

October

S	M	T	W	T	F	S
	1	2	3	4	5	6
7	8	9	10	11	12	13
14	15	16	17	18	19	20
21	22	23	24	25	26	27
28	29	30	31			

November

S	M	T	W	T	F	S
				1	2	3
4	5	6	7	8	9	10
11	12	13	14	15	16	17
18	19	20	21	22	23	24
25	26	27	28	29	30	

December

S	M	T	W	T	F	S
						1
2	3	4	5	6	7	8
9	10	11	12	13	14	15
16	17	18	19	20	21	22
23	24	25	26	27	28	29
30	31					

INTRODUCTION

Give it away—all of it—your cherished training secrets, your old running shoes, your time, your trophies, everything. It is in giving that runners gain. The sweat and hard work you leave on track or trail, even the hopes you bring to every workout, are only valuable when they're spent. It is the paradox of running that we are at our best when depleted.

You don't have to look far to find runners who are turning this paradox into a greater good. Lisa Shannon, an owner of a photography business in Portland, Oregon, listened in horror to an Oprah show one afternoon as a group of Congolese women spoke about the unthinkable violence perpetrated against them as a result of the conflict that has ravaged the Democratic Republic of Congo for 12 years. So Shannon sponsored two victims through Women For Women International (WFWI), a nonprofit organization that aids war refugees.

The effort seemed small, so she organized a 30-mile race and raised some $28,000, which bought everything from school fees to medical supplies for 80 refugees. Still feeling she could do more, she got noisy, putting up a Web site, badgering U.S. senators, and enlisting the help of other runners. When her second annual 30-mile run came around, Shannon had people in 10 states and four countries hosting their own Run for Congo Women events. Together, they raised more than $75,000.

It seemed only a matter of time before she would venture to the Congo in order to meet her beneficiaries—and to organize a race. With little communications infrastructure in the country, she traveled long distances across the savannah to meet them individually. Many had lost everything in the war, including their families. Even so, they constantly asked her, what can we do to support other women? Thus was born the first Run for Congo Women event in this war-torn region, against great odds. Insurgents still controlled much of the countryside. Women were in constant danger of rape and abduction. Shannon arranged for an all-woman police force for security and had many of the women racers transported the night before for safety. Races in Chicago, New York, and other places held in honor of the Congo event ultimately raised more than $47,000 and aided more than 33,000 women.

For some of us, giving it away signals a journey of discovery about how much grit we still have left inside. In 2005, New York City firefighter Matt Long finished an Ironman triathlon in 11 hours and a marathon that same year in just under three. Then he was hit and run over by a 20-ton bus, giving him a broken shoulder, leg, pelvis, foot, and assorted internal injuries. He was confined to a wheelchair and could manage only very short distances (to the bathroom, say) with a cane. But Long wanted to run again. In his gripping memoir, *The Long Run*, he recounts searching the country for a rehab clinic that understood this desire. He found one in Phoenix, and along with it, two lifelong friends.

If you've ever injured yourself in running, you know that rehab can be maddeningly slow. If you were never expected to walk again, rehab is essentially a prayer for a second life. The psychological journey is as torturous and frustrating as the physical healing. You realize early on that you can't do it without help. As Long describes it, his therapists Kyle and Mark "played coach, cheerleader, and dime-store psychologists. After a couple of weeks they also played hosts, taking me out with their wives for dinner." After many months, he ran his first mile in 17 minutes and 24 seconds, a time he used to turn in a 5K race. When he got back to his hotel, he called an old friend who had promised they'd run a six-mile course when he got back to New York. He told him to scrap those plans: "I'm doing the marathon," he reported.

Long learned the hard way, as many of us do, that the best we have within us often comes from others. In 2010, 16-year-old Holland Reynolds was a junior at San Francisco University High School. She had been a distance runner since the third grade, ending her freshman year as her school's fastest cross-country athlete. She credits her coach, Jim Tracy, 60, who arrived at University High School in 1994 and built both the girls' and boys' teams into perennial state champions. Tracy had a secret he couldn't hide for long: amyotrophic lateral sclerosis, or Lou Gehrig's disease. He began falling down during practice, bringing a chair to workouts, recognizing that his days as a coach and as a living man were running short. But the affection and loyalty his athletes held for him never wavered—especially Reynolds'.

At a state meet in Fresno in 2010, Reynolds was in third place at the 2.5-mile mark (of a 3.1-mile race). She was ready to make her move toward the lead of a 169-runner pack. But she suddenly felt confused. She slowed considerably and began to weave. Tracy knew something was terribly wrong when one of Reynolds' teammates crossed the finish line before her. And though he wears braces on his legs and his back, he lumbered out to the course in search of Reynolds. When he found her, their eyes locked, and she collapsed within two yards of the finish line. A race official ran out to tell her she needed only to get one foot across the finish line. It took her 17 seconds, but she crossed it— by crawling. She had more to give away than she ever knew.

A runner's calculus is time and miles, finish lines crossed, workouts completed. Through these we find the hard truths of what we can and cannot do. You'd think there would be a more humane measure of the faith and courage we bring to every race, to every workout. All runners know these are more essential than athletic gifts or ego. But since it can't be measured, sometimes you just have to see it. Look for it in people like Lisa Shannon, Matt Long, Jim Tracy, and Holland Reynolds.

—Marty Jerome ■

January

SUNDAY	MONDAY	TUESDAY	WEDNESDAY	THURSDAY	FRIDAY	SATURDAY
1 New Year's Day Kwanzaa ends (USA)	2 New Year's Day (observed) (Ireland, NZ, UK, Australia)	3 Bank Holiday (UK–Scotland)	4	5	6	7
8	9	10	11	12	13	14
15	16 Martin Luther King Jr.'s Birthday (observed) (USA)	17	18	19	20	21
22	23	24	25	26 Australia Day	27	28
29	30	31				

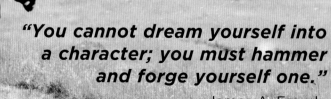

"You cannot dream yourself into a character; you must hammer and forge yourself one."

—James A. Froude

REACH

You will wake one bitter January morning as more or less the same runner you were in late December. So why does the dawn of a new year present a useful time to reassess your goals? There are far more constructive occasions: the day after a race; when the bathroom scale announces that you've shed (or gained) 10 pounds; the first workout in which you run 10K without stopping. Ah, but don't dismiss the calendar review. It shines light into the goals you already have. And January is as good as any month for doing it.

It could lead you to fatten them—your goals, that is. Personal drive narrows focus, a good thing because you're more likely to succeed when the purpose at hand is specific and realistic. Yet the miracle of training is that as you gain endurance, you also get faster; as you shed pounds, you get stronger; with confidence comes greater pleasure in running. At some point, newfound abilities deserve their own goals. It's okay to work on more than one thing at once.

Likewise, a January review may urge you to stretch your goals. Progress feels monumentally difficult in the early throes of a training program. Gains tend to build locomotive-like in the months that follow, accumulating faster than you probably anticipate. Even as your workouts are chuffing along rhapsodically with your goals, you shouldn't get too comfortable. A January review lets you grow ambition alongside roaring progress. It gives you permission to re-imagine yourself as a better runner.

It's also a good occasion to put your goals into therapy, to take a hard look at what's not working. Runners too often blame themselves for faltering results: poor discipline, waning zeal, whatever. More likely, the goals you've set aren't too high; they're just incongruous with who you are as an athlete. One way to get inside the head of your training program is to look at what gratifies you about your workouts— not the depleted glow you feel after you've showered or the confirming backslap of stopwatch results. Instead, look at the types of workouts and moments within them that genuinely lift your heart, that satisfy something besides your ego. Construe your goals from these things.

Or get rid of them altogether. At least, put them on ice. If your training program isn't working psychologically or otherwise, January is a splendid time to put a new routine to work, however temporarily. Just don't stop training entirely. You'll return to your original goals with new strengths and a sympathetic respect for where they're taking you. They'll be better informed. And if dedication and passion were truly your problems in realizing these ambitions, now you'll know it.

Of course, all this fussing over your training program may amount to nothing. That's okay, too. Your original goals may have been worthy targets all along. ∎

26 Monday

Where & When: Distance:

Comments:

27 Tuesday

Where & When: Distance:

Comments:

28 Wednesday

Where & When: Distance:

Comments:

29 Thursday

Where & When: Distance:

Comments:

30 Friday

Where & When: Distance:

Comments:

Dec 2011/Jan

Saturday 31

Where & When: Distance:

Comments:

1

Sunday 1

Where & When: Distance:

Comments:

© Stephen Matera/Aurora Photos/Corbis

tip: Intermediate goals—the ones that lead to your ultimate desires—are the true steppingstones of training. Pour your heart into these.

Distance this week: Weight:

Distance carried forward: _____

2 Monday   2

_____
_____
_____

Where & When: _____ **Distance:** _____
Comments: _____
_____

3 Tuesday   3

_____
_____
_____

Where & When: _____ **Distance:** _____
Comments: _____
_____

4 Wednesday   4

_____
_____
_____

Where & When: _____ **Distance:** _____
Comments: _____
_____

5 Thursday   5

_____
_____
_____

Where & When: _____ **Distance:** _____
Comments: _____
_____

6 Friday   6

_____
_____
_____

Where & When: _____ **Distance:** _____
Comments: _____
_____

January

Saturday 7

Where & When: _____ Distance: _____

Comments: _____

Sunday 8

Where & When: _____ Distance: _____

Comments: _____

© Pete Saloutos/Blend Images/Corbis

tip: Make the transition from treadmill to asphalt and concrete gradually. Your feet will thank you.

Distance this week: _____ Weight: _____

9 Monday

9

Where & When: Distance:

Comments:

10 Tuesday

10

Where & When: Distance:

Comments:

11 Wednesday

11

Where & When: Distance:

Comments:

12 Thursday

12

Where & When: Distance:

Comments:

13 Friday

13

Where & When: Distance:

Comments:

January

Saturday 14

4

Where & When: _____ Distance: _____

Comments: _____

Sunday 15

5

Where & When: _____ Distance: _____

Comments: _____

© Hannes Hepp/Corbis

tip: When switching from morning to evening runs—or vice versa—don't be surprised if performance lags. It can take up to two weeks for your body to adapt.

Distance this week: _____ Weight: _____

Distance carried forward:

16 Monday

16

Where & When: Distance:

Comments:

17 Tuesday

17

Where & When: Distance:

Comments:

18 Wednesday

18

Where & When: Distance:

Comments:

19 Thursday

19

Where & When: Distance:

Comments:

20 Friday

20

Where & When: Distance:

Comments:

January

Saturday 21

Where & When: Distance:
Comments:

Sunday 22

Where & When: Distance:
Comments:

© Erik Isakson/Tetra Images./Corbis

tip: If you're running to lose weight, aim to drop one to two pounds per week—no more. Otherwise, you may be burning muscle.

Distance this week: Weight:

Distance carried forward:

23 Monday   23

Where & When: Distance:

Comments:

24 Tuesday   24

Where & When: Distance:

Comments:

25 Wednesday   25

Where & When: Distance:

Comments:

26 Thursday   26

Where & When: Distance:

Comments:

27 Friday   27

Where & When: Distance:

Comments:

January

28

Where & When: Distance:

Comments:

29

Where & When: Distance:

Comments:

"Enjoy your body. Use it every way you can. Don't be afraid of it or of what other people think of it. It's the greatest instrument you'll ever own."

—Mary Schmich

tip: Old running shoes can teach you how to buy new ones. If the heels lean inward, you probably overpronate. If the upper toe is wrinkled, you likely need more motion control.

Notes:

Distance this week: **Weight:**

February

SUNDAY	MONDAY	TUESDAY	WEDNESDAY	THURSDAY	FRIDAY	SATURDAY
			1	2	3	4
5	6 Waitangi Day (NZ)	7	8	9	10	11
12	13	14 St. Valentine's Day	15	16	17	18
19	20 Presidents' Day (USA)	21	22 Ash Wednesday	23	24	25
26	27	28	29			

"Success isn't permanent, and failure isn't fatal."
—Mike Ditka

VALENTINE

Think of the selfish workout, the one you take by casting rightful priorities aside. Running is a brilliant procrastinator. It's a splendid way to hide—from your boss or spouse, from diaper duty or the nightly news. It lets you pretend you're serving a higher cause (your spiritual well being, your gorgeous butt). Most of us recognize when we're shirking from life and loved ones with a run, even if it's part of our weekly routine. So what to do with all that guilt?

Reject it. Honestly, take an inventory of all that running gives back to those who matter in your life, and consider it a valentine. You will never convince loved ones that your running does them a favor, of course, and making the case will seem disingenuous. So it's best to show it, not sell it. Those who know you will recognize how the benefits of your training shower into their lives as well—in household tranquility, in your health and self-confidence, and in the private joy that running radiates to everything around you.

This doesn't mean there won't be tetchy moments in negotiating your workouts, especially when a race date looms. And though training for an event takes meticulous planning, it can be done months in advance, with only minor tweaks to shore up progress. Begin talking up the event as early as possible. Get everyone on board, including work colleagues. Convey its personal importance to them. Do not renege on any commitment you've made outside of your workouts. And be gracious about unwelcome surprises—especially funerals, work emergencies, and illnesses. Consistent training brings cumulative strength. Losing a week of running isn't much of a setback.

Rejecting guilt about your selfish workouts doesn't free you from listening to the clamor of complaints about them, especially when those clamoring have a point. All runners should periodically review the value they place on training. Workouts can be hideouts, not only from other people, but also from depression, professional adversity, or a drifting marriage. Running, like just about anything else, can turn into a crippled obsession, the signs unapparent until blowups at work or home make it clear. Self-honesty about training requires ongoing appraisal. It's not a one-time admission.

Of course, getting philosophical about something as fundamentally primitive as running may seem silly. We all know why we run—our objectives and the results. Less obvious is the way that running describes us as individuals, in the ways that others see us. Workouts, even when we do them in groups, are wholly personal endeavors. In this sense, they're always selfish. They can blind us to the changes that others see in us. So when someone speaks up about your training, have the good sense to listen.

And be willing to give back where you can. The only thing a workout truly steals from others is time. With a little mutual understanding, the rewards can be shared. ■

30 Monday 30

Where & When: Distance:

Comments:

31 Tuesday 31

Where & When: Distance:

Comments:

1 Wednesday 32

Where & When: Distance:

Comments:

2 Thursday 33

Where & When: Distance:

Comments:

3 Friday 34

Where & When: Distance:

Comments:

January/February

Saturday 4

Where & When: **Distance:**

Comments:

Sunday 5

Where & When: **Distance:**

Comments:

© Sam Diephuis,/Corbis

tip: Don't confuse mental fatigue with physical fatigue. A hard run after a long day will give both brain and body renewed energy.

Distance this week: **Weight:**

Distance carried forward:

6 Monday 37

Where & When: Distance:

Comments:

7 Tuesday 38

Where & When: Distance:

Comments:

8 Wednesday 39

Where & When: Distance:

Comments:

9 Thursday 40

Where & When: Distance:

Comments:

10 Friday 41

Where & When: Distance:

Comments:

February

Saturday 11

Where & When: Distance:

Comments:

Sunday 12

Where & When: Distance:

Comments:

tip: Ten minutes on a treadmill will raise sufficient body temperature—and courage—to face the bitter cold that awaits you outside.

© Jenny Gaulitz/Johnér Images/Corbis

Distance this week: **Weight:**

13 Monday 44

Where & When: Distance:

Comments:

14 Tuesday 45

Where & When: Distance:

Comments:

15 Wednesday 46

Where & When: Distance:

Comments:

16 Thursday 47

Where & When: Distance:

Comments:

17 Friday 48

Where & When: Distance:

Comments:

February

Saturday 18

Where & When: Distance:

Comments:

Sunday 19

Where & When: Distance:

Comments:

© Erik Isakson/Corbis

tip: Nearly all runners and cyclists understand that when you bark, "on your left!" it means you're passing them. But it can confuse hikers, strollers, and children. Go wide around them.

Distance this week: **Weight:**

Distance carried forward:

20 Monday 51

Where & When: Distance:

Comments:

21 Tuesday 52

Where & When: Distance:

Comments:

22 Wednesday 53

Where & When: Distance:

Comments:

23 Thursday 54

Where & When: Distance:

Comments:

24 Friday 55

Where & When: Distance:

Comments:

February

Saturday 25

Where & When: Distance:

Comments:

Sunday 26

Where & When: Distance:

Comments:

"There are really only three types of people: those who make things happen, those who watch things happen, and those who ask, what happened?"

—Ann Landers

tip: If you run on a track, periodically switch directions (if local etiquette allows), so that you don't overdevelop your outer leg.

Notes:

Distance this week: Weight:

March

SUNDAY	MONDAY	TUESDAY	WEDNESDAY	THURSDAY	FRIDAY	SATURDAY
				1 St. David's Day (UK)	2	3
4	5 Labour Day (Australia—WA)	6	7	8 Purim* International Women's Day	9	10
11	12 Eight Hours Day (Australia—TAS) Labour Day (Australia—VIC) Canberra Day (Australia—ACT) Commonwealth Day (Australia, Canada, NZ, UK)	13	14	15	16	17 St. Patrick's Day
18 Mothering Sunday (Ireland, UK)	19	20	21	22	23	24
25	26	27	28	29	30	31

*Begins at sundown the previous day

"Don't let what you cannot do interfere with what you can do."

—John Wooden

QUITTING

You don't want an ambulance ride to put an end to running. You don't even want your doctor to prescribe it. And it's more than mortal danger that should force every runner to contemplate the dreadful business of quitting.

It defies our instincts. Running improves our health and fills us with vitality. Why on earth would we stop? Our very identities are often invested in it, a signal element in how others perceive who we are. Our egos are also at work, especially if we compete. And if we train with others—a group, a friend, a loved one—a cherished connection is at stake.

Yet health and happiness bring risks with every workout. Our limitations as athletes are revealed with a mile marker or a stopwatch; the perils of desire and dedication require blunt self-honesty and philosophical calculation. Heart disease typically does that honest and calculating thing for you, especially if you're male and over the age of 35. Much murkier are the repetitive running injuries, the chronic pain, and minor disabilities that nag at daily living. There's also a psychological time to quit, when you're not getting the results you want and perhaps, without admitting it, you hate your workouts.

The thing about quitting is that it need not be final, especially if you're nursing an injury or waiting for the spark to return. It requires strategy. Many running injuries are vindictive in the ways they seemingly vanish and then return with fury when you resume your old workouts. They should be given more healing time than seems humanly fair. While you wait, you'll want to maintain your aerobic base by switching to a less punishing form of training. This transition presents marvelous opportunity in new abilities and forms of satisfaction waiting to be discovered. Many runners who could never see themselves otherwise find that a bicycle, a swimming pool, or a racquetball court reveals an athlete that exceeded their imaginations. Many never return to running. So experiment. Make the time as rich as possible.

If you don't convert to another sport, an overhaul is in order in how you run. Scrutinize everything about your routine—your shoes, your course, your partners, how you cross train, the time of day you work out, and anything else that may have led you to quit. Be prepared for surprises. Work shoes, not running shoes, are often the culprit for running injuries. You're more likely to be hurt in a morning workout. There's a world of difference between asphalt and concrete in the pounding your body takes.

Equally important to how you run is why. Quitting is an excellent time to reflect on what you seek from training and to summon the courage to change. The beauty of training is that there are multiple ways of meeting your goals, of rediscovering passion. Sometimes you have to simply stop in order to find out if the love was real. ∎

27 Monday   58

Where & When: Distance:
Comments:

28 Tuesday   59

Where & When: Distance:
Comments:

29 Wednesday   60

Where & When: Distance:
Comments:

1 Thursday   6

Where & When: Distance:
Comments:

2 Friday   62

Where & When: Distance:
Comments:

February/March

Saturday 3

Where & When: Distance:

Comments:

Sunday 4

Where & When: Distance:

Comments:

© ImageShop/Corbis

tip: Face it: You're going to miss a run from time to time. Pay attention to patterns of lapsed training, not on individual workouts.

Distance this week: Weight:

Distance carried forward:

5 Monday 65

Where & When: Distance:

Comments:

6 Tuesday 66

Where & When: Distance:

Comments:

7 Wednesday 67

Where & When: Distance:

Comments:

8 Thursday 68

Where & When: Distance:

Comments:

9 Friday 69

Where & When: Distance:

Comments:

March

Saturday 10

Where & When: Distance:

Comments:

Sunday 11

Where & When: Distance:

Comments:

© Erik Isakson/Tetra Images/Corbis

tip: A racing heart rate when you're completely at rest may signal overtraining.

Distance this week: Weight:

Distance carried forward: _____

12 Monday   72

_____

_____

_____

Where & When: _____ **Distance:** _____

Comments: _____

_____

13 Tuesday   73

_____

_____

_____

Where & When: _____ **Distance:** _____

Comments: _____

_____

14 Wednesday   74

_____

_____

_____

Where & When: _____ **Distance:** _____

Comments: _____

_____

15 Thursday   75

_____

_____

_____

Where & When: _____ **Distance:** _____

Comments: _____

_____

16 Friday   76

_____

_____

_____

Where & When: _____ **Distance:** _____

Comments: _____

_____

77

Where & When: **Distance:**

Comments:

78

Where & When: **Distance:**

Comments:

© Mike Kemp/Rubberball/Corbis

tip: Your training schedule should be written in pencil, not pen. Progress and setbacks should periodically bring it up for revision.

Distance this week: **Weight:**

19 Monday 79

Where & When: **Distance:**

Comments:

20 Tuesday 80

Where & When: **Distance:**

Comments:

21 Wednesday 81

Where & When: **Distance:**

Comments:

22 Thursday 82

Where & When: **Distance:**

Comments:

23 Friday 83

Where & When: **Distance:**

Comments:

84

Where & When: Distance:

Comments:

85

Where & When: Distance:

Comments:

© Stefanie Grewel/Corbis

tip: Whenever you wonder whether a driver sees you, assume that he doesn't.

Distance this week: **Weight:**

26 Monday

86

Where & When: Distance:

Comments:

27 Tuesday

87

Where & When: Distance:

Comments:

28 Wednesday

88

Where & When: Distance:

Comments:

29 Thursday

89

Where & When: Distance:

Comments:

30 Friday

90

Where & When: Distance:

Comments:

March/April

Saturday 31

Where & When: **Distance:**

Comments:

Sunday 1

Where & When: **Distance:**

Comments:

"I'm not going to run this again."
—Grete Waitz, after winning her first of nine New York City Marathons

tip: If you can walk a very steep grade faster than you can run it, walk. It conserves time and energy.

Notes:

Distance this week: **Weight:**

April

SUNDAY	MONDAY	TUESDAY	WEDNESDAY	THURSDAY	FRIDAY	SATURDAY
1 Palm Sunday	2	3	4	5	6 Good Friday (Western)	7 Passover* Easter Saturday (Australia—except TAS, WA)
8 Easter (Western)	9 Easter Monday (Australia, Canada, Ireland, NZ, UK—except Scotland)	10	11	12	13 Holy Friday (Orthodox)	14 Passover ends
15 Easter (Orthodox)	16	17	18	19	20	21
22 Earth Day	23 St. George's Day (UK)	24	25 Anzac Day (NZ, Australia)	26	27	28
29	30					

*Begins at sundown the previous day

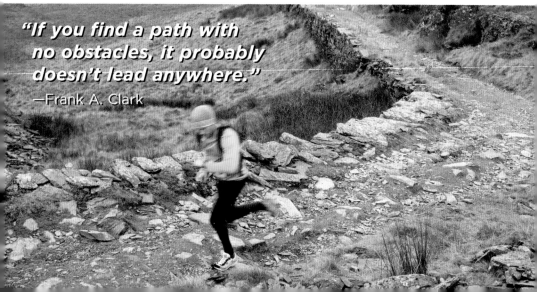

"If you find a path with no obstacles, it probably doesn't lead anywhere."

—Frank A. Clark

MUD

If you've never done it, it's easy to believe that trail running is all about dreamy communion with the natural scenery. Quite the opposite: It demands fierce concentration, a maddening darting of focus from the scree and mud beneath your feet to the switchbacks and hills on the horizon, which will affect your pace and test your determination. This bifurcated concentration is the joy of it. And sure, there are often nice things to see.

Pacing on a trail tends to bewilder those transitioning from tracks and roads, certainly because of the extreme changes that any particular route may demand, but also because you have far less control over your workouts. Even flat, dry fire roads can turn into speed-sapping glop after a day of rain. The time it takes you to complete the same distance on the same trail can vary dramatically, not only season to season, but also day to day. At first you must begrudgingly accept this truth, but over time, you'll come to treasure the liberation from the stopwatch. Trail running forces you to measure your talents as an athlete in more varied ways.

It will also force you to develop more varied muscle groups. Your quads, the muscles just north of your knees, will take grueling punishment from steep descents and from any leaping you do. But they'll also get strong. Pelvic and hip muscles provide stability over uneven surfaces. Core strength training helps. And over time, you will discover muscles in your feet and above your ankles you never knew existed.

Look for changes in your form as well: a shorter stride to maintain your center of gravity; shoulders relaxed with arms raised slightly so that you can use them winglike for balance over uneven surfaces; and your head bent slightly forward so that eyes can cut to the horizon or to the six or seven paces in front of you, depending on the terrain. Face plants and butt skids are the least of your worries for balance. The more serious perils are twisted ankles and ripped muscles.

The skills required to negotiate trails will accrue naturally over time. They're fun. In short order, intuition will tell you when you can hurdle a fallen tree or a stream. Rocks come loose under foot on descents, so you will instinctively try to land on dirt. Even racers walk (or climb) up sheers and very steep grades. The firm sand at the bank of a fast-moving creek or river typically gives better footing than outlying mud. By the way, dry feet are a treasure. If you must forge water early in your run, be willing to sacrifice a little time to find a hospitable crossing. And it's okay to use a fallen branch as a temporary crutch across a log or narrow ravine. Trail running requires equal measures of imagination and determination.

With your mind so frenetically preoccupied with changing terrain, how do you enjoy the natural splendor? This eventually becomes second nature. ∎

Distance carried forward: _____

2 Monday 93

_____
_____
_____

Where & When: _____ **Distance:** _____
Comments: _____
_____

3 Tuesday 94

_____
_____
_____

Where & When: _____ **Distance:** _____
Comments: _____
_____

4 Wednesday 95

_____
_____
_____

Where & When: _____ **Distance:** _____
Comments: _____
_____

5 Thursday 96

_____
_____
_____

Where & When: _____ **Distance:** _____
Comments: _____
_____

6 Friday 97

_____
_____
_____

Where & When: _____ **Distance:** _____
Comments: _____
_____

April

Saturday 7

Where & When: Distance:

Comments:

Sunday 8

Where & When: Distance:

Comments:

© Ty Milford/Aurora Open/Corbis

tip: Trail runners: A whistle may be more effective (and easier to carry) than a cell phone for seeking emergency help in areas where signals are weak or nonexistent.

Distance this week: Weight:

9 Monday 100

Where & When: Distance:

Comments:

10 Tuesday 101

Where & When: Distance:

Comments:

11 Wednesday 102

Where & When: Distance:

Comments:

12 Thursday 103

Where & When: Distance:

Comments:

13 Friday 104

Where & When: Distance:

Comments:

105

Saturday 14

Where & When: Distance:

Comments:

106

Sunday 15

Where & When: Distance:

Comments:

© Jordan Siemens/Aurora Photos/Corbis

tip: A bright orange cap or vest tells hunters that you're not dashing prey asking to be field dressed and barbecued.

Distance this week: Weight:

16 Monday 107

Where & When: Distance:

Comments:

17 Tuesday 108

Where & When: Distance:

Comments:

18 Wednesday 109

Where & When: Distance:

Comments:

19 Thursday 110

Where & When: Distance:

Comments:

20 Friday 111

Where & When: Distance:

Comments:

112

Where & When: Distance:

Comments:

113

Where & When: Distance:

Comments:

© Ty Milford/Aurora Open/Corbis

tip: Running in sand improves your leg turnover rate. It also builds supporting muscles in ankles and feet.

Distance this week: Weight:

Distance carried forward:

23 Monday 114

Where & When: Distance:
Comments:

24 Tuesday 115

Where & When: Distance:
Comments:

25 Wednesday 116

Where & When: Distance:
Comments:

26 Thursday 117

Where & When: Distance:
Comments:

27 Friday 118

Where & When: Distance:
Comments:

119

Where & When: Distance:
Comments:

120

Where & When: Distance:
Comments:

"Character—the willingness to accept responsibility for one's own life—is the source from which self-respect springs."

—Joan Didion

tip: Go ahead and run the descent part of a hill fast. It improves leg turnover rate, which you'll appreciate in late-breaking sprints at the end of a race or long workout.

Notes:

Distance this week: Weight:

May

SUNDAY	MONDAY	TUESDAY	WEDNESDAY	THURSDAY	FRIDAY	SATURDAY
		1	2	3	4	5
6	7 Labour Day (Australia—QLD) May Day (Australia—NT) Early May Bank Holiday (Ireland, UK)	8	9	10	11	12
13 Mother's Day (USA, Australia, Canada, NZ)	14	15	16	17	18	19 Armed Forces Day (USA)
20	21 Victoria Day (Canada)	22	23	24	25	26
27	28 Memorial Day (USA) Spring Bank Holiday (UK—Scotland)	29	30	31		

"Training is principally an act of faith."

—Franz Stampfl, coach to Roger Bannister

MILEAGE

As they say, your long run puts the tiger in the pussycat. It's hard to keep that in mind once you discover speed drills. The miraculous benefits that intervals, hill charges, tempo runs, and the like confer on any training program come quick and sure. For half the investment of time, they make you stronger and faster. They also bring variety to your workouts, urging you to explore, mix it up, and learn.

By contrast, the long run is an exercise in plodding drudgery. How did you ever come to love running if distance was your introduction? Alas, it's how we all came to love running. And if you're new or returning, it is the foundation on which everything else must be built. You have no choice. It is your best insurance against injury. Years after you've run the same distance at the same pace, it continues to improve the efficiency and strength of the machinery that pushes you down the road. Your splashy speed drills would be impossible without it.

Even when you're at the peak of fitness, your long run continues to build heart strength and lung capacity, albeit with smaller returns. The work it does for muscles needs no disclaimer. Your long grinding workouts ceaselessly develop the latticework of blood capillaries, which pipe oxygen into remote tissues and slog waste products out. They increase the density of mitochondria in your cells, the biological spark plugs that transform the energy from pork chops and pasta into speed and endurance. And they train your body to burn fat over glycogen, which saves the latter for a fast kick at the end of a race (or to propel you through speed drills).

Bear in mind that your long run doesn't have to be long. For some, it can be as little as three miles. When you're starting over, measure it by time, not by distance. Raise it by 10 percent every other week. Once you switch to distance, don't be a mule to mileage. There will be long months when you can't budge its limits. And maybe you shouldn't. Plateaus are inevitable, and it's a mistake to view them as setbacks. As long as you meet the last distance you ran, you will continue to build the athlete within.

So what is the ideal mileage? Obviously, your training goals will lead you to it, but try to be Goldilocks: Seek a distance that is not too long, not too fast, and not too easy. You can still mix it up. Walk breaks are welcome, especially when you're pushing mileage you never thought possible. Progression runs, in which you start very slow and gradually build speed, dispel monotony. They force you to think about pace. Like no other drill, they will teach you to recognize your personal limits, when you can run through the pain and when you can't. On the other side of that pain, however you cope with it, your body will tenderly remind you to love your long run. ∎

Distance carried forward:

30 Monday 121

Where & When: Distance:
Comments:

1 Tuesday 122

Where & When: Distance:
Comments:

2 Wednesday 123

Where & When: Distance:
Comments:

3 Thursday 124

Where & When: Distance:
Comments:

4 Friday 125

Where & When: Distance:
Comments:

126

Saturday 5

Where & When: **Distance:**

Comments:

127

Sunday 6

Where & When: **Distance:**

Comments:

© Brian Bailey/CORBIS

tip: All distance runners can improve their efficiency by adding resistance training to their workouts.

Distance this week: **Weight:**

Distance carried forward: _____

7 Monday 128
_____
_____
_____

Where & When: _____ **Distance:** _____
Comments: _____

8 Tuesday 129
_____
_____
_____

Where & When: _____ **Distance:** _____
Comments: _____

9 Wednesday 130
_____
_____
_____

Where & When: _____ **Distance:** _____
Comments: _____

10 Thursday 131
_____
_____
_____

Where & When: _____ **Distance:** _____
Comments: _____

11 Friday 132
_____
_____
_____

Where & When: _____ **Distance:** _____
Comments: _____

May

Saturday 12

Where & When: **Distance:**

Comments:

Sunday 13

Where & When: **Distance:**

Comments:

© Cathrine Wessel/CORBIS

tip: If your legs hurt the day after your weekly long run, you're likely running it too fast, not too long.

Distance this week: **Weight:**

14 Monday
135

Where & When: Distance:

Comments:

15 Tuesday
136

Where & When: Distance:

Comments:

16 Wednesday
137

Where & When: Distance:

Comments:

17 Thursday
138

Where & When: Distance:

Comments:

18 Friday
139

Where & When: Distance:

Comments:

140

Where & When: **Distance:**

Comments:

141

Where & When: **Distance:**

Comments:

© Monalyn Gracia/Corbis

tip: Most streets and road shoulders are cambered so that water won't pool in the center. This can cause you to pronate, inviting injury over time. Seek the flattest surfaces possible.

Distance this week: **Weight:**

21 Monday   142

Where & When: Distance:

Comments:

22 Tuesday   143

Where & When: Distance:

Comments:

23 Wednesday   144

Where & When: Distance:

Comments:

24 Thursday   145

Where & When: Distance:

Comments:

25 Friday   146

Where & When: Distance:

Comments:

147

Where & When: **Distance:**

Comments:

148
Sunday 27

Where & When: **Distance:**

Comments:

© Jakob Helbig/cultura/Corbis

tip: Don't worry about lagging in the middle of a run. Your body is probably switching its fuel from carbohydrates to fat. You'll usually get a second wind.

Distance this week: **Weight:**

28 Monday 149

Where & When: Distance:
Comments:

29 Tuesday 150

Where & When: Distance:
Comments:

30 Wednesday 151

Where & When: Distance:
Comments:

31 Thursday 152

Where & When: Distance:
Comments:

1 Friday 153

Where & When: Distance:
Comments:

154

Saturday 2

Where & When: Distance:

Comments:

155

Sunday 3

Where & When: Distance:

Comments:

"It is true that speed kills. In distance running, it kills anyone who does not have it."

—Brooks Johnson

tip: A marathon is not ideal for a first race. Too many things can go wrong and you may not know how to recover. Shorter races make great rehearsals.

Notes:

Distance this week: Weight:

June

SUNDAY	MONDAY	TUESDAY	WEDNESDAY	THURSDAY	FRIDAY	SATURDAY
					1	2
3	4 Queen's Birthday (NZ) Foundation Day (Australia—WA) Spring Bank Holiday (Ireland, UK—except Scotland)	5 Diamond Jubilee Holiday (UK)	6	7	8	9
10	11 Queen's Birthday (Australia—except WA)	12	13	14 Flag Day (USA)	15	16
17 Father's Day (USA, Canada, Ireland, UK)	18	19	20	21	22	23
24	25	26	27	28	29	30

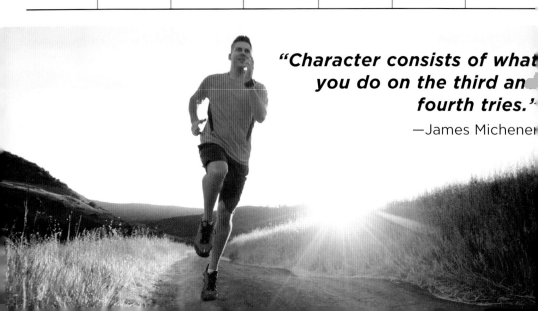

"Character consists of what you do on the third and fourth tries."

—James Michener

DRUNK

Thirst is a fool. Sure, it's a critical messenger from your body, but the sensation is a besotted and hapless courier. It arrives after your body is already dehydrated, lingers too long, and gives off all manner of bad information. You'd as well ignore it completely, except that it can occasionally save your life.

It certainly shouldn't direct your workouts. Running requires long-range scheming for hydration—and here's why: A gulp of Gatorade doesn't instantly slake your body, even if it quenches your thirst. Any liquid you drink must be processed through your stomach, into your intestines, on through your kidneys, and into your bloodstream, where it is then expurgated as sweat. This business takes hours. It is the slow boat to Tangiers, and you can't rush it with biological bribes.

Even so, your body adapts to hot weather over time. As summer temperatures climb north, your blood plasma, the holding tank for sweat, begins to store up water. To be sure, it takes its time—usually ten days to two weeks. Marathoners who jet in from chilly climes to a tropical race with hopes they can adapt in three days by doing sit-ups in the hotel sauna typically find a rude surprise. The sunny news is that your body's adaptation to hot weather doesn't necessarily entail training. Puttering in the garden, long leisurely walks, or even dinner al fresco under a late-afternoon broil will eventually set a runner right for summer.

In calculating how to hydrate before a race or a workout, math is more reliable than thirst, sort of. Here's the medical consensus: Multiply your weight by 0.08. That's how much liquid (in ounces) you need each day just to replenish what the summer's simmer takes away. For training, you should weigh yourself—yes, butt naked—before a run. Weigh yourself again after the run. Every pound of weight lost in the workout equals roughly 16 ounces of liquid you need to store up beforehand. Trouble is, you can't just gulp it down by the ounce, cup in hand, since much of the liquid we consume every day comes from food, which is impossible to calculate.

Suddenly, the math gets woozy. And you become thirstier when you drink anything with sugars in it. What's a runner to do? Here's the obvious but neglected solution: Go slowly into the heat. When temperatures spike, drink throughout the day, not just in the hours leading up to a race or a workout. Remember that caffeine and alcohol are diuretics. Air conditioning and high altitudes can dry you out. Bear in mind that the symptoms of dehydration are often subtle. Headaches and muscle cramps are signals. So is an inexplicable slump in your normal running pace. Look for these signs as dangers, but muster the patience to let your body adapt. Also, when your pace and spirit lag, it sometimes helps to ask, am I thirsty? ■

4 Monday   156

Where & When: Distance:

Comments:

5 Tuesday   157

Where & When: Distance:

Comments:

6 Wednesday   158

Where & When: Distance:

Comments:

7 Thursday   159

Where & When: Distance:

Comments:

8 Friday   160

Where & When: Distance:

Comments:

161

Where & When: Distance:

Comments:

162

Where & When: Distance:

Comments:

© Alex Mares-Manton/Asia Images/Corbis

tip: Is your dog suffering heat exhaustion on your run? Whining and a tongue that hangs low and round at the tip should tell you to knock off and seek water.

Distance this week: Weight:

Distance carried forward:

11 Monday 163

Where & When: Distance:

Comments:

12 Tuesday 164

Where & When: Distance:

Comments:

13 Wednesday 165

Where & When: Distance:

Comments:

14 Thursday 166

Where & When: Distance:

Comments:

15 Friday 167

Where & When: Distance:

Comments:

June

Saturday 16

Where & When: Distance:

Comments:

Sunday 17

Where & When: Distance:

Comments:

© Dave and Les Jacobs/Blend Images/Corbis

tip: Dehydration on a distance run is often the culprit for an unexpected slow pace.

Distance this week: **Weight:**

18 Monday170

Where & When: Distance:

Comments:

19 Tuesday171

Where & When: Distance:

Comments:

20 Wednesday172

Where & When: Distance:

Comments:

21 Thursday173

Where & When: Distance:

Comments:

22 Friday174

Where & When: Distance:

Comments:

175   **Saturday 23**

Where & When: **Distance:**

Comments:

176   **Sunday 24**

Where & When: **Distance:**

Comments:

© RCWW, Inc./Corbis

tip: Pre-hydrating before a race or long run? You're smart. Begin drinking one to two hours beforehand—eight to 16 ounces will do it.

Distance this week: **Weight:**

Distance carried forward:

25 Monday 177

Where & When: **Distance:**

Comments:

26 Tuesday 178

Where & When: **Distance:**

Comments:

27 Wednesday 179

Where & When: **Distance:**

Comments:

28 Thursday 180

Where & When: **Distance:**

Comments:

29 Friday 181

Where & When: **Distance:**

Comments:

182 · **Saturday 30**

Where & When: _____ Distance: _____

Comments: _____

183 · **Sunday 1**

Where & When: _____ Distance: _____

Comments: _____

"Mental will is a muscle that needs exercise, just like the muscles of the body."

—Lynn Jennings, nine-time winner of USA Cross Country Championships

tip: For a long run on a hot day, fill your water bottle half way, freeze it, and then top it off with water.

tip: Not only are temperatures cooler in the mornings, but your body's core temperature is lower as well.

Notes: _____

_____

_____

_____

Distance this week: _____ **Weight:** _____

July

SUNDAY	MONDAY	TUESDAY	WEDNESDAY	THURSDAY	FRIDAY	SATURDAY
1 Canada Day	2	3	4 Independence Day (USA)	5	6	7
8	9	10	11	12	13	14
15	16	17	18	19	20 Ramadan	21
22	23	24	25	26	27	28
29	30	31				

"Bid me run, and I will strive with things impossible."
—Shakespeare

WOMEN

For more than 40 years, the running world has treated women athletes as soft and petite versions of men. Coaching, sports physiology research, athletic apparel—even the ways competitive events are organized—have proceeded unwaveringly from the assumption that all runners stand up when they pee. But this scientific evidence just in: You're not a man!

Your foot strike is different. In fact, your feet are different. So is the geometry of your legs and knees and hips (as if nobody noticed). You heal from sports injuries in ways we're only beginning to understand. You metabolize food differently. Yet here we are, deep in the new millennium—with Paula Radcliffe and Deena Kastor and women's world records toppling everywhere—still stuck in the male idea of what running should be.

The glacial pace of change is depressing, but not surprisingly, inroads are coming first from academia. Take knee injuries, especially the dreaded ACL tears, which afflict women runners far more commonly than men. Why? The distance between a woman's knees and feet is shorter than a man's, her ankles are more flexed, and her feet roll outward more. This affects foot strike. Men suffer the same problem when they're fatigued, but women begin with the disadvantage. The takeaway is that women must be more vigilant about fatigue. When it's time to stop, stop.

Likewise, sports physiologists have known for years that protein aids in recovery after a hard workout, at least for those who think a college beer-can collection is a work of art. Women have rarely been invited into such studies. Finally, we're discovering that protein doesn't have the same benefit for females. On the other hand, estrogen offers a superior and still-mysterious protection for muscles after the wear and tear of a hard workout. Women recover more quickly from long runs, no need for a self-congratulatory steak dinner.

Carbo-loading, sacrosanct to marathoners, delivers less benefit to women than to men. It's the best insurance against bonking on any long run for both sexes, but females should bring greater strategy to refueling along the way. Meanwhile, women can take satisfaction that their bodies switch into a fat-burning mode more quickly than the opposite sex. You'll work off your butt faster than he'll work off his gut.

Apparel makers have been more attentive to women runners, thanks to the vast profits that have blossomed from the running boom. Shoemakers now deftly understand the unique architecture of the female foot—offering more flexible midsoles, wider foot beds, and thinner heels. Bra makers have been slower to innovate. Many women aren't keenly thrilled with the fit of bras they wear to work, never mind the sports variety. Today's running bras certainly improve on the early 1970s, in which two jockstraps stitched together promised all the support a woman could want. Even so, they haven't come a long way, baby. ■

Distance carried forward:

2 Monday 184

Where & When: Distance:

Comments:

3 Tuesday 185

Where & When: Distance:

Comments:

4 Wednesday 186

Where & When: Distance:

Comments:

5 Thursday 187

Where & When: Distance:

Comments:

6 Friday 188

Where & When: Distance:

Comments:

189

Where & When: Distance:

Comments:

Sunday 8

190

Where & When: Distance:

Comments:

© Artiga Photo/Corbis

tip: Running with a jogging stroller impedes natural arm swing, so push with one arm and swing the other. Intermittently switch arms.

Distance this week: Weight:

9 Monday 191

Where & When: Distance:

Comments:

10 Tuesday 192

Where & When: Distance:

Comments:

11 Wednesday 193

Where & When: Distance:

Comments:

12 Thursday 194

Where & When: Distance:

Comments:

13 Friday 195

Where & When: Distance:

Comments:

Saturday 14

Where & When: Distance:

Comments:

Sunday 15

Where & When: Distance:

Comments:

© Steve Prezant /Corbis

tip: High heels can lead to plantar fasciitis and Achilles tendinopathy in runners. If you must wear them, remove them often and stretch your calf muscles.

Distance this week: Weight:

Distance carried forward:

16 Monday 198

Where & When: Distance:

Comments:

17 Tuesday 199

Where & When: Distance:

Comments:

18 Wednesday 200

Where & When: Distance:

Comments:

19 Thursday 201

Where & When: Distance:

Comments:

20 Friday 202

Where & When: Distance:

Comments:

Saturday 21

203

Where & When: Distance:

Comments:

---

204   **Sunday 22**

Where & When: Distance:

Comments:

© Take A Pix Media/Tetra Images/Corbis

tip: The best time to run along the beach is at low tide when you can seek out packed sand.

Distance this week: Weight:

Distance carried forward:

23 Monday 205

Where & When: Distance:

Comments:

24 Tuesday 206

Where & When: Distance:

Comments:

25 Wednesday 207

Where & When: Distance:

Comments:

26 Thursday 208

Where & When: Distance:

Comments:

27 Friday 209

Where & When: Distance:

Comments:

Saturday 28

Where & When: Distance:

Comments:

Sunday 29

Where & When: Distance:

Comments:

"Running is my meditation, mind flush, cosmic telephone, mood elevator, and spiritual communion."
—Lorraine Moller, Bronze winner, 1992 Olympics

tip: Do competitors give you anxiety? Celebrate them. Remind yourself that you're running with the best.

Notes:

Distance this week: Weight:

August

SUNDAY	MONDAY	TUESDAY	WEDNESDAY	THURSDAY	FRIDAY	SATURDAY
			1	2	3	4
5	6 Summer Bank Holiday (Ireland, UK–Scotland, Australia–NSW) Picnic Day (Australia–NT)	7	8	9	10	11
12	13	14	15	16	17	18
19 Eid al-Fitr	20	21	22	23	24	25
26	27 Summer Bank Holiday (UK–except Scotland)	28	29	30	31	

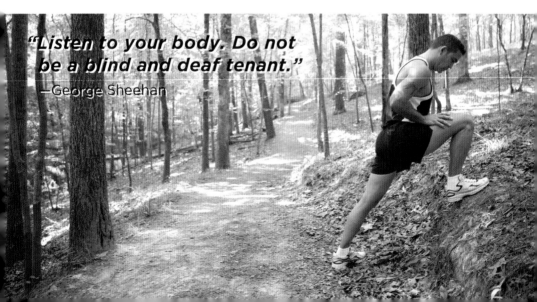

"Listen to your body. Do not be a blind and deaf tenant."
—George Sheehan

PAIN

One persistent myth about elite athletes is that they don't hurt as much as you do. If you race, there will inevitably come a devastating day when you are at the very limits of what your body can endure, only to watch an elite runner sweep by as if carried by angels. It's dumbfounding. How do they withstand the agony? The truth is that no one feels your pain. Like love and fear, the sensation is universal, but the burden or blessing is entirely personal.

Training itself extends the threshold for suffering. Your body produces endorphins and other chemicals that inhibit pain. But these play less of a role than previously thought. Recent research shows that it's not that you hurt less when you're in peak fitness; it's that pain has become familiar. It has become your running partner, for better and worse. You know the throb in your hip will dissipate when you get past mile two. You know that your muscles always burn at certain parts of your workout, but that relief follows quickly afterward. Uncertainty gives pain its psychological advantage.

Coaches will tell you that runners who are familiar with a race course will turn in faster times while reporting less pain. On your regular workout route, you may feel as if your calves are ripping on the ascent of a long hill. But you also know the hill will eventually crest, and if you've run it dozens of times before, you can be satisfied that it won't defeat you. You've put pain in its place.

There are numerous psychological strategies for coping with agony. Most would have you focus on your running goals—both immediate (make it to that grove of poplar trees ahead), and long term (run the company 10K race in the spring). Some elite marathoners will tell you that in the final miles of a race they will turn their attention to the cheering crowds, a reminder of why they race. This is a form of dissociation: intentionally distracting your thoughts from the pain. And there's danger in it.

When you ignore how much you hurt, pace often becomes erratic. You tend to speed up, only to hit a physiological wall that forces you to slow down. It's an inefficient way to run. It squanders energy. And in a race, it can throw you off your game. More importantly, pain is an ongoing conversation your body is having with the runner in your head. It's trying to protect you. There is risk of injury in every step of every workout, and the ways you suffer help you calculate the odds.

Trouble is, pain is a nagging and inarticulate conversant. It's often hard to interpret it. But here are key reasons to quit for the day: Any sharp, sudden pain that worsens as you run should send you home. Limping is your body's way of quieting the agony that results from some form of injury. Chest pains should always raise alarms. Vomiting isn't good, either. ∎

Distance carried forward:

30 Monday   212

Where & When: Distance:

Comments:

31 Tuesday   213

Where & When: Distance:

Comments:

1 Wednesday   214

Where & When: Distance:

Comments:

2 Thursday   215

Where & When: Distance:

Comments:

3 Friday   216

Where & When: Distance:

Comments:

July/August

Saturday 4

Where & When: **Distance:**

Comments:

Sunday 5

Where & When: **Distance:**

Comments:

© Tomas Rodriguez/Corbis

tip: Head off injury. With unfamiliar pain, stop all speed work and dial back distance. Gradually bring these back to your workouts.

Distance this week: **Weight:**

6 Monday 219

Where & When: **Distance:**

Comments:

7 Tuesday 220

Where & When: **Distance:**

Comments:

8 Wednesday 221

Where & When: **Distance:**

Comments:

9 Thursday 222

Where & When: **Distance:**

Comments:

10 Friday 223

Where & When: **Distance:**

Comments:

August

Where & When: **Distance:**

Comments:

Where & When: **Distance:**

Comments:

© Artiga Photo/Corbis

tip: When returning from injury, lose the headphones. Music can divert your attention from residual pain you should be heeding.

Distance this week: **Weight:**

Distance carried forward: _____

13 Monday   226

_____
_____

Where & When: _____ **Distance:** _____
Comments: _____
_____

14 Tuesday   227

_____
_____

Where & When: _____ **Distance:** _____
Comments: _____
_____

15 Wednesday   228

_____
_____

Where & When: _____ **Distance:** _____
Comments: _____
_____

16 Thursday   229

_____
_____

Where & When: _____ **Distance:** _____
Comments: _____
_____

17 Friday   230

_____
_____

Where & When: _____ **Distance:** _____
Comments: _____
_____

August

231

Where & When: _____   Distance: _____

Comments: _____

Sunday 19

232

Where & When: _____   Distance: _____

Comments: _____

© Image Source/Corbis

tip: When injury forces you into cross training, continue with it after you've healed. Gradually scale it back.

Distance this week: _____   Weight: _____

Distance carried forward:

20 Monday 233

Where & When: Distance:

Comments:

21 Tuesday 234

Where & When: Distance:

Comments:

22 Wednesday 235

Where & When: Distance:

Comments:

23 Thursday 236

Where & When: Distance:

Comments:

24 Friday 237

Where & When: Distance:

Comments:

August

Saturday 25

Where & When: Distance:

Comments:

Sunday 26

Where & When: Distance:

Comments:

© Clarissa Leahy/cultura/Corbis

tip: With any pain that worsens through a run or that alters your gait, take three days off. On the fourth day, run half your normal distance at a much slower pace.

Distance this week: **Weight:**

27 Monday   240

Where & When: Distance:
Comments:

28 Tuesday   241

Where & When: Distance:
Comments:

29 Wednesday   242

Where & When: Distance:
Comments:

30 Thursday   243

Where & When: Distance:
Comments:

31 Friday   244

Where & When: Distance:
Comments:

Aug/Sept

Saturday 1

Where & When: Distance:

Comments:

Sunday 2

Where & When: Distance:

Comments:

"If an athlete ever admits to being ready for competition, without the slightest injury, raring to go and sure to win, you know it's time to send for the jacket with the laces up the back."

—Pat Butcher, British journalist

tip: RICE—rest, ice, compression, elevation—is the best known runner's first aid for pain or injury. But don't delay. It's most effective when applied immediately.

Notes:

Distance this week: Weight:

September

SUNDAY	MONDAY	TUESDAY	WEDNESDAY	THURSDAY	FRIDAY	SATURDAY
						1
2	3	4	5	6	7	8
Father's Day (Australia, NZ)	Labor Day (USA, Canada)					
9	10	11	12	13	14	15
16	17	18	19	20	21	22
	Rosh Hashanah*	Rosh Hashanah ends			U.N. International Day of Peace	
23	24	25	26	27	28	29
30			Yom Kippur*			

*Begins at sundown the previous day

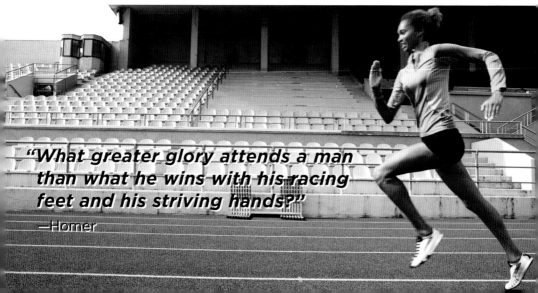

"What greater glory attends a man than what he wins with his racing feet and his striving hands?"
—Homer

RACER

Don't let anyone talk you out of the marathon. Millions of people would never run at all were it not for that solemn, grand ambition. Simply completing one can be the achievement of a lifetime. But know this: Shorter races teem with as much tribal excitement. Training for them gets you in better shape. You can also have a life outside of workouts.

Better still, you don't have to choose one over the other. In fact, shorter races are invaluable for rehearsing a marathon—the starting-line jitters, pacing, working your way through a pack, hydrating and fueling, keeping your competitive cool, and putting on a fast kick to the finish line. Training for them is different, however. Some of the benefits are synergistic; others won't help you at all in a 26.2-mile event.

A 5K race makes a splendid icebreaker for competition, especially for the psychology and planning required at the starting line. Because they're quick, you don't have time to warm up or find your pace; you have to arrive prepared. You can get by with a relatively light four- to seven-mile weekly long run. The rest of your workouts must be concentrated on speed drills (400- and 800-meter intervals are ideal). These will give you fast finishes in longer events, but they won't aid in much else. There's simply no substitute for workout mileage if you want to race long distances.

A 10K event is one of the most competitive amateur events you'll find, combining grinding endurance with speed. Many racers go out too fast, and it's easy to let their competitive drive affect your own pace. You'll pay for it in the end. Training for a 10K race entails a pleasing variety of distance and speed work. A weekly long run of six to eight miles is mandatory. Otherwise, 1K repeats and tempo runs will get you to the starting line. The key is to build an innate sense of the pace you can sustain. Training for a 10K builds a foundation for a marathon, should you burn to enter one, but you'll need to begin adding miles at least three months before the longer event.

The half marathon (13.1 miles) is terribly underrated for the courage it requires and for the competitive satisfaction it brings to mortals and average runners. Many coaches insist that you enter one before attempting its double-distance cousin. Training is essentially the same for both events: Mileage matters. The good news is that you can put both races within relatively close range on the calendar. Planning is crucial for both your long-range training and tapering schedule, as well as race-day plotting about fuel, water, and pace.

The distance you choose demands more than a little self-knowledge, beginning with your abilities as a runner. You should look also at your motivations. Racing is an organizing principle for training, demarcated by a date on a calendar and a moment of truth. The event itself often matters less than how you get there. ∎

Distance carried forward:

3 Monday   247

Where & When: Distance:

Comments:

4 Tuesday   248

Where & When: Distance:

Comments:

5 Wednesday   249

Where & When: Distance:

Comments:

6 Thursday   250

Where & When: Distance:

Comments:

7 Friday   251

Where & When: Distance:

Comments:

September

Saturday 8

Where & When: Distance:

Comments:

Sunday 9

Where & When: Distance:

Comments:

© Olix Wirtinger/Corbis

tip: Not ready for a marathon? Many events now offer relay options that divide the distance into four or five legs. Run a leg . . . or two.

Distance this week: **Weight:**

Distance carried forward: _____

10 Monday 254

_____

Where & When: _____ Distance: _____

Comments: _____

11 Tuesday 255

_____

Where & When: _____ Distance: _____

Comments: _____

12 Wednesday 256

_____

Where & When: _____ Distance: _____

Comments: _____

13 Thursday 257

_____

Where & When: _____ Distance: _____

Comments: _____

14 Friday 258

_____

Where & When: _____ Distance: _____

Comments: _____

September

Saturday 15

Where & When: Distance:

Comments:

Sunday 16

Where & When: Distance:

Comments:

© Motofish Images/Corbis

tip: If you don't have the steam for a fast finish, don't panic. Focus on picking off individual runners.

Distance this week: **Weight:**

17 Monday 261

Where & When: Distance:
Comments:

18 Tuesday 262

Where & When: Distance:
Comments:

19 Wednesday 263

Where & When: Distance:
Comments:

20 Thursday 264

Where & When: Distance:
Comments:

21 Friday 265

Where & When: Distance:
Comments:

September

Saturday 22

Where & When: _____ Distance: _____

Comments: _____

Sunday 23

Where & When: _____ Distance: _____

Comments: _____

© Stock Foundry/Design Pics/Corbis

tip: If you've got jitters leading up to your first race, lose your time goals. You're already going to set a personal record.

Distance this week: _____ **Weight:** _____

24 Monday   268

Where & When: Distance:

Comments:

25 Tuesday   269

Where & When: Distance:

Comments:

26 Wednesday   270

Where & When: Distance:

Comments:

27 Thursday   271

Where & When: Distance:

Comments:

28 Friday   272

Where & When: Distance:

Comments:

September

273   **Saturday 29**

Where & When: Distance:

Comments:

274   **Sunday 30**

Where & When: Distance:

Comments:

"So many people crossing the finish line of a marathon look as happy as when I won. They have tears in their eyes. This sport is full of winners."
—Gary Muhrcke, champion of the inaugural New York City Marathon, 1970

tip: Runners come to the triathlon with an advantage: It's easier (and faster) to ramp up to swimming and cycling than it is to running.

Notes:

Distance this week: Weight:

October

SUNDAY	MONDAY	TUESDAY	WEDNESDAY	THURSDAY	FRIDAY	SATURDAY
	1 Labour Day (Australia—ACT, NSW, SA) Queen's Birthday (Australia—WA)	2	3	4	5	6
7	8 Columbus Day (USA) Thanksgiving (Canada)	9	10	11	12	13
14	15	16	17	18	19	20
21	22 Labour Day (NZ)	23	24 United Nations Day	25	26 Eid al-Adha	27
28	29 Bank Holiday (Ireland)	30	31 Halloween			

"To travel hopefully is better than to arrive."
—Sir James Jeans

FEAST

Ignore your appetite. This is hard for runners to hear—we, who are so attuned to the marvels of physical existence. Most of us relish a hearty meal after a workout, just as we enjoy a hot shower, a sound night's sleep, and the pleasing tug of our calf muscles as we ascend a flight of stairs. Runners inhabit the physical world more fully than sedentary types. We have learned to trust our bodies with abandon. Why be suspicious of hunger?

Blame it on human design. Appetite is an oafish signal, arriving too late and offering almost no specific guidance about what your body needs in order to thrive. You'd as well eat your socks when the first surges of hunger strike. Little by little, we're learning what runners need, yet too often, the books, magazines, and Web sites take a scientific principle and extrapolate from it what you should put in your mouth at this very moment. Nine months later you'll read that such advice was utter hooey all along.

You know you need more calories when you're training. But how many, what types, and when do you eat them? The evidence is confounding. It depends on your age, your gender, your base metabolism rate, your height and weight, and probably, the weather. It's no information at all. The same is true of carbohydrate loading. Plenty of evidence suggests it works, but the results you get depend on your unique body. We know that protein helps rebuild muscles torn during workouts, and some running coaches urge their athletes to consume protein shakes immediately after a run. Some nutritionists, on the other hand, believe there's too much of it in our diets to begin with. And what about vitamins and minerals?

It's maddening. And those who run to control weight have it worst of all. Add some resistance training to your regular run, and you may see your waist slim down even as the bathroom scale shoots north. Why? Muscle weighs more than fat. And if you're restricting calories at the same time you're adding miles to your workouts, you're probably a cranky bear around loved ones. How long can you maintain your regimen without losing friends, your sanity, or your spouse?

It would be easy enough to throw up your hands, except that sports nutrition can be brought to earth with three general principles. Those who push highly specific dietary advice on you (eat this oat bar exactly two hours before your workout) don't know what they're talking about. Discover for yourself what works. That's the first principle. Here's the second: Stay ahead of your appetite at all times. Hunger pains will remind you that you skipped lunch at work. In a distance race, you'll just bonk, game over. It's infuriating. Finally, eat a well-balanced diet, just as your mother told you. Take pleasure in your meals. It is one of the sweet perks of being a runner. Just make sure you finish your broccoli. ∎

1 Monday   275

Where & When: Distance:
Comments:

2 Tuesday   276

Where & When: Distance:
Comments:

3 Wednesday   277

Where & When: Distance:
Comments:

4 Thursday   278

Where & When: Distance:
Comments:

5 Friday   279

Where & When: Distance:
Comments:

280

Where & When: **Distance:**

Comments:

281

Where & When: **Distance:**

Comments:

© Image Source/Corbis

tip: Pacing your calorie intake during a distance event can be as important as pacing your speed. Rehearse it in your workouts.

Distance this week: **Weight:**

Distance carried forward:

8 Monday 282

Where & When: Distance:

Comments:

9 Tuesday 283

Where & When: Distance:

Comments:

10 Wednesday 284

Where & When: Distance:

Comments:

11 Thursday 285

Where & When: Distance:

Comments:

12 Friday 286

Where & When: Distance:

Comments:

October

Saturday 13

Where & When: Distance:

Comments:

Sunday 14

Where & When: Distance:

Comments:

© Artiga Photo/Corbis

tip: If heartburn (acid reflux) often strikes you on long runs, eat two small meals instead of one large one beforehand. And cut out coffee, chocolate, and citrus.

Distance this week: Weight:

Distance carried forward:

15 Monday   289

Where & When: Distance:

Comments:

16 Tuesday   290

Where & When: Distance:

Comments:

17 Wednesday   291

Where & When: Distance:

Comments:

18 Thursday   292

Where & When: Distance:

Comments:

19 Friday   293

Where & When: Distance:

Comments:

294 _____ **Saturday 20**

_____

_____

_____

Where & When: _____ Distance: _____

Comments: _____

_____

295 _____ **Sunday 21**

_____

_____

_____

Where & When: _____ Distance: _____

Comments: _____

_____

© Ocean/Corbis

tip: Runners need more protein than nonrunners. Beans and grains are great for a complete source, but contrary to popular belief, you don't need to eat them at the same meal.

Distance this week: _____ Weight: _____

Distance carried forward:

22 Monday   296

Where & When: Distance:
Comments:

23 Tuesday   297

Where & When: Distance:
Comments:

24 Wednesday   298

Where & When: Distance:
Comments:

25 Thursday   299

Where & When: Distance:
Comments:

26 Friday   300

Where & When: Distance:
Comments:

October

Saturday 27

Where & When: Distance:

Comments:

Sunday 28

Where & When: Distance:

Comments:

"Ambition leads me not only farther than any other man has been before me, but as far as I think it possible for man to go."

—James Cook

tip: Ginger has anti-inflammatory compounds that can reduce joint pain. It's great in a stir-fry, dessert, or tea.

tip: Caffeine before a run can reduce asthma symptoms.

Notes:

Distance this week: Weight:

November

SUNDAY	MONDAY	TUESDAY	WEDNESDAY	THURSDAY	FRIDAY	SATURDAY
				1	2	3
4	5	6 Election Day (USA)	7	8	9	10
11 Veterans' Day (USA) Remembrance Day (Canada, Ireland, UK)	12 Veterans' Day (observed) (USA)	13	14	15	16	17
18	19	20	21	22 Thanksgiving (USA)	23	24
25	26	27	28	29	30 St. Andrew's Day (UK)	

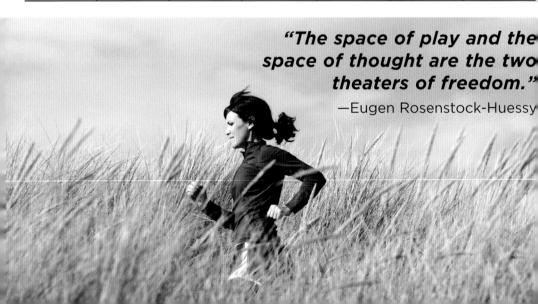

"The space of play and the space of thought are the two theaters of freedom."

—Eugen Rosenstock-Huessy

SPICE

Cross training is often forced on runners by injury, which impugns it as a kind of therapeutic slum, an ignoble detention hall from your truest athletic ambitions. This characterization isn't unfair. If you want to get stronger as a runner, you have to run. Swimming, weight training, cycling, aerobics classes, and weekend tennis games all shower benefits on a runner, but not many. Sorry about that. Some of these activities even work against you. And indeed, they steal time from reaching your running goals.

Before you dismiss it, however, consider the subtler values of cross training, which come wrapped around the principle of pleasure. Everyone's running program becomes tyrannical from time to time. Cross training is a way of managing it, of restoring equanimity, of shedding new light and fresh possibility into the things that urged you to buy that first pair of running shoes. Cross training rehabilitates the running program as well as the runner. Along the way, you may discover a life-lasting passion.

You don't have to injure yourself to benefit from it. All runners should periodically dial back their training schedules—certainly after a distance race, but also after steady months of hard training. Like it or not, your body needs a holiday so that it can mend through and through. Inclement seasons present a fine opportunity to dump half your regular mileage and introduce cross training (indoor?), which maintains muscle mass and aerobic fitness. Whatever time of year you do it, returning to your old peak mileage will be faster and far less painful.

Cross training also provides refuge when your training program turns against you, physically and otherwise. Call it a performance plateau (or trough); progress stalls. Harder workouts and higher mileage yield . . . nothing. The force of will and hard work fails to budge you, sometimes for months on end. Or worse—you've gone stale. You vaguely dread your next workout, plod through it, and begin to find more pressing matters to shoo it off your weekly schedule. All runners endure these periods. Cross training forces you to see anew your athletic talents and limitations. It often kicks up solutions. Failing that, it can lead you to new goals. And on the psychology front, it dispels the monotony that sacks many running programs. It shakes them up, even if it ultimately takes you to a new sport.

Usually it doesn't. Nobody embraces running, love at first sight. Likewise, you shouldn't view cross training as a betrayal, so much as a way of stepping up your game. Coaches will tell you that core strength training from weights improves the efficiency of a good running form. Basketball and tennis strengthen ankles, which prevents running injuries. Cycling and swimming build aerobic fitness without a punishing impact. And the list goes on. Our bodies are a single apparatus, not just a pair of legs attached to a cardiovascular pump and the desire of a marathoner. Improving one part doesn't take away from the others. ■

Distance carried forward:

29 Monday 303

Where & When: Distance:

Comments:

30 Tuesday 304

Where & When: Distance:

Comments:

31 Wednesday 305

Where & When: Distance:

Comments:

1 Thursday 306

Where & When: Distance:

Comments:

2 Friday 307

Where & When: Distance:

Comments:

308 _____ **Saturday 3**

_____

_____

_____

Where & When: _____ **Distance:** _____

Comments: _____

_____

309 _____ **Sunday 4**

_____

_____

_____

Where & When: _____ **Distance:** _____

Comments: _____

_____

© Image Source/Corbis

tip: When doing strength training or yoga, use a mirror to check that you're working the right muscles.

Distance this week: _____ **Weight:** _____

Distance carried forward: _____

5 Monday   310

_____
_____
_____

Where & When: _____ **Distance:** _____
Comments: _____
_____

6 Tuesday   311

_____
_____
_____

Where & When: _____ **Distance:** _____
Comments: _____
_____

7 Wednesday   312

_____
_____
_____

Where & When: _____ **Distance:** _____
Comments: _____
_____

8 Thursday   313

_____
_____
_____

Where & When: _____ **Distance:** _____
Comments: _____
_____

9 Friday   314

_____
_____
_____

Where & When: _____ **Distance:** _____
Comments: _____
_____

November

Saturday 10

Where & When: Distance:

Comments:

Sunday 11

Where & When: Distance:

Comments:

© Roy McMahon/Corbis

tip: For cross training, the elliptical provides the best biomechanical simulation of running. But swimming, cycling, resistance exercises, and rowing machines build strength in muscles that running neglects.

Distance this week: **Weight:**

Distance carried forward:

12 Monday 317

Where & When: **Distance:**

Comments:

13 Tuesday 318

Where & When: **Distance:**

Comments:

14 Wednesday 319

Where & When: **Distance:**

Comments:

15 Thursday 320

Where & When: **Distance:**

Comments:

16 Friday 321

Where & When: **Distance:**

Comments:

November

322

Where & When: Distance:

Comments:

323

Sunday 18

Where & When: Distance:

Comments:

© Steve Hix/Somos Images/Corbis

tip: Beware of the "terrible toos"—doing too much, too soon, too fast. Your body needs time to adapt.

Distance this week: **Weight:**

Distance carried forward:

19 Monday 324

Where & When: Distance:

Comments:

20 Tuesday 325

Where & When: Distance:

Comments:

21 Wednesday 326

Where & When: Distance:

Comments:

22 Thursday 327

Where & When: Distance:

Comments:

23 Friday 328

Where & When: Distance:

Comments:

November

Saturday 24

Where & When: Distance:

Comments:

Sunday 25

Where & When: Distance:

Comments:

© Purestock/SuperStock/Corbis

tip: Balance training, in which you have to maintain your equilibrium while working with weights, builds your inner-most abdominals. They make your running form more efficient.

Distance this week: **Weight:**

Distance carried forward:

26 Monday   331

Where & When: Distance:

Comments:

27 Tuesday   332

Where & When: Distance:

Comments:

28 Wednesday   333

Where & When: Distance:

Comments:

29 Thursday   334

Where & When: Distance:

Comments:

30 Friday   335

Where & When: Distance:

Comments:

Nov/Dec

Saturday 1

Where & When: Distance:

Comments:

Sunday 2

Where & When: Distance:

Comments:

"Road racing is rock and roll; track is Carnegie Hall"
—Marty Liquori, third American high schooler to beat the four-minute mile

tip: Practice your finishing kick in workouts that are shorter than your race distance. It will give you confidence in your pace.

Notes:

Distance this week: Weight:

December

SUNDAY	MONDAY	TUESDAY	WEDNESDAY	THURSDAY	FRIDAY	SATURDAY
						1
2	3	4	5	6	7	8
9	10	11	12	13	14	15
Hanukkah*	Human Rights Day					
16	17	18	19	20	21	22
Hanukkah ends						
23	24 Christmas Eve	25 Christmas Day	26 Kwanzaa begins (USA) Boxing Day (Canada, UK, NZ, Australia—except SA) St. Stephen's Day (Ireland) Proclamation Day (Australia—SA)	27	28	29
30	31					

*Begins at sundown the previous day

"No great thing is created suddenly."
—Epictetus

OLDSTER

One gift of getting older—and there aren't many—is that you begin to take the long view. Try convincing a high-school track star that he'll trash his knees by training in flats on concrete, and you'll probably get a dismissive smirk. After all, he's getting results. Offer a workout tip to a middle-aged marathoner, and you're likely to start a conversation.

All runners strive for breakthroughs, departure points that unleash the better runner within. You have to suppose that older runners sooner recognize the mirages, but all ages are duped from time to time by hope and hard work. Time and training resolve these matters; in the meantime, your goals owe you some respect. Every workout should proceed from the premise that you'll be running 10 years from now, not just 10 weeks. Goals should adjust accordingly.

This is particularly difficult when a race date glares at you from the calendar. Experienced runners know that cramming doesn't work, but they also know that unbridled desire (and a little adrenalin) can occasionally make miracles. It hurts to scratch a race date because you're unprepared, more painful still to face a workout the next day. Suck it up. Humiliation and injury hurt worse, and there will always be other events.

Youthful enthusiasm will also let you down. We've all had periods of sustained training in which the gains seem torrential and ceaseless. The feeling is glorious. The urge is to pile on ever more miles, squeeze in more workouts, oblivious that we're stepping off a cliff. Sorry to contradict the listen-to-your-body crowd, but a 10 percent rule will better help you to train into your dotage: Don't increase mileage or intensity by more than 10 percent every two weeks, even when your exultant body wants more.

The same is true of speed training, whether it's intervals, hill charges, tempo runs, or anything else. We all need them in our workouts, even come to love the stupendous gains they deliver, heedless about how they can turn on us. Get twice the results for half the mileage. Why not add more—or work them harder? You've seen this movie before, and you know that it ends with injury. More than any part of your training program, speed work demands a healthy respect. Know when to back off. Give your body plenty of time to recover.

And here's a tip that whippersnappers hate: To avoid injury, shorten your stride. Eight chronic running afflictions are now tied to overstriding, an exuberant excess of the pugnaciously competitive . . . and youth. You probably don't even recognize when you're doing it. Besides setting you up for harm, it decreases your running efficiency, putting you on a fast boat to exhaustion. With a shorter stride, you land softer, with less impact to the rest of the apparatus. Of course, you lose speed, which means that your workouts will need to focus on a quicker turnover rate.

A final tip for older runners: ice. Use it generously. It works. Honestly it does. ■

Distance carried forward: _____

3 Monday
338

_____
_____
_____

Where & When: _____ **Distance:** _____
Comments: _____

4 Tuesday
339

_____
_____
_____

Where & When: _____ **Distance:** _____
Comments: _____

5 Wednesday
340

_____
_____
_____

Where & When: _____ **Distance:** _____
Comments: _____

6 Thursday
341

_____
_____
_____

Where & When: _____ **Distance:** _____
Comments: _____

7 Friday
342

_____
_____
_____

Where & When: _____ **Distance:** _____
Comments: _____

December

Saturday 8

Where & When: Distance:

Comments:

Sunday 9

Where & When: Distance:

Comments:

© Jeremy Woodhouse/Blend Images./Corbis

tip: Chin up: When your head droops, you're blocking oxygen flow.

Distance this week: **Weight:**

Distance carried forward:

10 Monday 345

Where & When: Distance:

Comments:

11 Tuesday 346

Where & When: Distance:

Comments:

12 Wednesday 347

Where & When: Distance:

Comments:

13 Thursday 348

Where & When: Distance:

Comments:

14 Friday 349

Where & When: Distance:

Comments:

December

Saturday 15

Where & When: _____ Distance: _____

Comments: _____

Sunday 16

Where & When: _____ Distance: _____

Comments: _____

© Stock Foundry/Design Pics/Corbis

tip: A shower before a race warms muscles, preparing them for work.

Distance this week: _____ **Weight:** _____

17 Monday 352

Where & When: Distance:
Comments:

18 Tuesday 353

Where & When: Distance:
Comments:

19 Wednesday 354

Where & When: Distance:
Comments:

20 Thursday 355

Where & When: Distance:
Comments:

21 Friday 356

Where & When: Distance:
Comments:

December

357

Where & When: _____ Distance: _____
Comments: _____

358

Where & When: _____ Distance: _____
Comments: _____

© David Foster/Blend Images/Corbis

tip: When running into a hard wind, try to draft behind another runner.
It's not cheating and it will help you conserve energy.

Distance this week: _____ **Weight:** _____

Distance carried forward:

24 Monday   359

Where & When: Distance:
Comments:

25 Tuesday   360

Where & When: Distance:
Comments:

26 Wednesday   361

Where & When: Distance:
Comments:

27 Thursday   362

Where & When: Distance:
Comments:

28 Friday   363

Where & When: Distance:
Comments:

December

Saturday 29

Where & When: **Distance:**

Comments:

Sunday 30

Where & When: **Distance:**

Comments:

© Ocean/Corbis

tip: Snow-covered roads and trails are safe if you slow your pace.
But ice? Hit the treadmill.

Distance this week: **Weight:**

Distance carried forward:

31 Monday

366

Where & When: **Distance:**
Comments:

1 Tuesday

Where & When: **Distance:**
Comments:

2 Wednesday

Where & When: **Distance:**
Comments:

3 Thursday

Where & When: **Distance:**
Comments:

4 Friday

Where & When: **Distance:**
Comments:

Dec/Jan 2013

Saturday 5

Where & When: _____ Distance: _____

Comments: _____

Sunday 6

Where & When: _____ Distance: _____

Comments: _____

"Time is the enemy. Time is what we are fighting in our lives, as we fight it in our running. We can never achieve a total victory, but every time we achieve a partial one . . . we affirm our human dignity."

—Coach Sam Dee, *The Olympian*

tip: Can you train for a race from a treadmill? Not advised. The machine keeps your pace; you may struggle to find it on race day.

Notes: _____

_____

_____

_____

Distance this week: _____ **Weight:** _____

Twelve Months of Running

Jan. 2	Jan. 9	Jan. 16	Jan. 23	Jan. 30	Feb. 6	Feb. 13	Feb. 20	Feb. 27	March 5	March 12	March 19	March 26

To create a cumulative bar graph of weekly mileage,
apply an appropriate scale at the left-hand margin.
Then fill in the bar for each week of running.

Apr. 2	Apr. 9	Apr. 16	Apr. 23	Apr. 30	May 7	May 14	May 21	May 28	June 4	June 11	June 18	June 25

To create a cumulative bar graph of weekly mileage,
apply an appropriate scale at the left-hand margin.
Then fill in the bar for each week of running.

July 2	July 9	July 16	July 23	July 30	Aug. 6	Aug. 13	Aug. 20	Aug. 27	Sept. 3	Sept. 10	Sept. 17	Sept. 24

To create a cumulative bar graph of weekly mileage,
apply an appropriate scale at the left-hand margin.
Then fill in the bar for each week of running.

| Oct. 1 | Oct. 8 | Oct. 15 | Oct. 22 | Oct. 29 | Nov. 5 | Nov. 12 | Nov. 19 | Nov. 26 | Dec. 3 | Dec. 10 | Dec. 17 | Dec. 24 |

A Record of Races

Date	Place	Distance	Time	Pace	Comments & Excuses

A Record of Races

Date	Place	Distance	Time	Pace	Comments & Excuses

JANUARY 2013
_____
_____
_____
_____
_____
_____

FEBRUARY 2013
_____
_____
_____
_____
_____
_____

MARCH 2013
_____
_____
_____
_____
_____
_____

APRIL 2013
_____
_____
_____
_____
_____
_____

MAY 2013
_____
_____
_____
_____
_____
_____

JUNE 2013
_____
_____
_____
_____
_____
_____

JULY 2013
_____
_____
_____
_____
_____
_____

AUGUST 2013
_____
_____
_____
_____
_____
_____

SEPTEMBER 2013
_____
_____
_____
_____
_____
_____

OCTOBER 2013
_____
_____
_____
_____
_____
_____

NOVEMBER 2013
_____
_____
_____
_____
_____
_____

DECEMBER 2013
_____
_____
_____
_____
_____
_____